Peace In Kind

Words to me from God and Jesus

to Share with You

RICHARD PARNES

WRITERS'
BRANDING

Peace In Kind:
Words to me from God and Jesus to Share with You
Copyright © 2023 by Richard Parnes

ISBN:

Paperback: 978-1639456321
e-book: 978-1639456338

Writers' Branding
1-800-608-6550
www.writersbranding.com
media@writersbranding.com

Table of Contents

Note about the Cover Painting:

Forty plus years ago, I met the artist, Ms. Vicars, who showed me her paintings in her studio in Los Angeles. When I saw the painting now on the cover of this collection of words, I told her that I saw the "beauty of Heaven and everlasting splendor." I told her it was magnificent, in my eyes and opinion, of which I did not really believe was worth anything. Upon hearing how I felt, she promptly took the painting and handed it to me saying she wanted me to have it as a gift. I was totally amazed and asked if she was sure she wanted me to have it. She said that…

…**"No one else had seen the vision she felt she saw when she painted it."**

It now hangs in my home where anyone who visits can see. I feel blessed to have this wonderful piece of art in my home. Each time I look at it, I become relaxed and seem to stare further into its depth. I find myself searching for more time to enjoy this remarkable and extraordinary piece of work and a deeper relationship with the Holy Trinity.

—Richard Parnes

To the Reader:

When I first decided to put the words to paper, they were all written with one goal in mind; to give thanks, acknowledgement and praise to God Almighty and the Lord Jesus Christ. Over the past years, I have listened to the words come into my mind through prayer and meditation. I know that I am being spoken to, contacted by, and any other processes dealing with what I believe are my angels, teachers and guides, for a reason.

I try to ascertain that which is good and that which is negative and immediately negate the negative for the positive. It is important to understand and rise to a higher level and hear what words need to be chosen. I also realize that I am just a vessel being used to fill empty pages.

While many may not believe in the process, or may even state opinions which contradict how my writings were perceived, this is obviously a choice all writers are subject. The goal is to present and allow for the contemplation of the words to be either enjoyed or criticized accordingly. I also realize that I am not the first person to do this.

I wish to thank my wife for having the patience and love to see me complete this collection.

—Richard Parnes

(Author's note: if you feel while reading that there is a rhythm coming into your mind, you would not be alone. As I was writing, I also was able to put the words to music. Some of the titles have a double ** next to them. This signifies that the music associated was composed by Brenda Smith of Southern California. Her talent was pivotal throughout.)

When Love is all Around

When love is all around,
There will be peace on earth.
All of the troubled past will fade a timely death.
When love is all around,
Harmony fills the air,
Mankind will live as one.
Gone is the deep despair.
I can see a rich clear sky of rainbows passing, colors fly
Into the heavens up above.
There's glory in a world of love.

When love is all around,
Hunger no longer stays.
Feeding a needy world, mankind will earn the praise.
When love is all around,
Peace will embrace the earth.
War is a foreign word,
Giving a new rebirth.
I can vision countries far all working towards a distant star.
To build respect for all that is,
A universal land of bliss.

When love is all around,
We will no longer hate.
Gender will cease to strive, equally, before the gate.
When love is all around,
Forgiveness a daily trend.
Karma will only be good
to the very end.
I can hear a chorus sing, a wedding song, a golden ring
Of cultures mixing without pause.
There's only room. Expand the cause.

When love is all around, peace will be sung.
Peace will be sung.
Mankind has won.
Mankind has won.

We Will Be Free

You don't need another dollar.
You don't need another car.
You don't need two houses to live in.
Don't you know who you really are?
But you need the Lord above you.
And you need His only Son.
And you need the words that he gave you.
Believe He's the only One.
'Cause Jesus, He's our savior.
If we confess all our sins,
He is faithful and so righteous to forgive all the wrong that
we did.

Now we travel without thinking.
We pollute the world He gave.
And the day passes without a care,
Can't you see we'll be in our grave?
So pray to the Lord above you
And bless His holy name.
For if we don't thank Him for His glorious deeds,
Our lives will be in vain.
And Jesus gave His life for us
And we need to clean up our act.
'Cause redemption's coming. We need to listen. Our lives
should be intact.

So listen carefully, Jesus is on His way.
Don't sin constantly.
Thank the Lord. Bless His name.
And we will be free.
Remember the commandments that Moses brought down
And study prophesy.
Jesus, He's our savior and we will be free.

You don't need another dollar.
You don't need another car.
You don't need two houses to live in.
Don't you know who you really are?
But you need the Lord above you.
And you need His only Son.
And you need the words that he gave you.
Believe He's the only One.
'Cause Jesus, He's our savior.
If we confess all our sins,
He is faithful and so righteous to forgive all the wrong that
we did.
Jesus is our savior. We will be free.

Peace in Kind**

Lost and alone I find myself in…
Need of that someone to just be content with…
Only a prayer I call on the one who is my friend.
Hungry and cold no shelter to walk in…
Bothered and troubled no bed I can sleep in…
Seeking the light in the night I'll go to no end.

Silently He speaks to me.
Rests assured my mind.
Takes away the hurt inside,
Peace in Kind.
Lets me know his graciousness.
Forever we will bind.
His unending love will not unwind.
Peace in Kind.

Slowly I find myself in a dream with…
Angels that take me and show me a team where…
Calmness and beauty engulf all the sorrows that once were me.
Touching His hand He tells me to walk to…
Only a place where love will embrace through…
All of the moments I thought I would never see.

Silently he speaks to me.
Rests assured my mind.
Takes away the hurt inside,
Peace in Kind.
Lets me know his graciousness.
Forever we will bind.
His unending love will not unwind.
Peace in Kind.

An Inspiration True

Doesn't matter now
What the world thinks of me
I only care for
The afterlife I seek
Whether I'm to stay
And finish what began
The loved ones I'll leave
Will pick up where I stand

The teachers will inspire
Continue on with truth
Watch with loving eyes
His words go on as proof
Developing their souls
Go on and to inspire
There's nothing more to give
And nothing to require

This is my love
I'll always remember you
Jesus you're the One
An inspiration true

The strength you exude
The hurt that you feel
You pick the pieces up
Rewards are your zeal

The small but gifted group
The promises and vows
The work will go on
Don't question why or how

This is my love
I'll always remember you
Jesus you're the One
An inspiration true
This is my love
I'll always remember you
Jesus you're the One
An inspiration true

Just Listen**

Paths I had taken in haste were the narrow roads to go.
I should have followed my heart for He is there I know.
So let me listen…Just really Listen.
The Lord will tell me…Which road to go.

For He is there in the spotlight,
And my feet will travel His light
to the kingdom of the chosen.
The ones He's blessed
But there are few who will listen…
To the golden words well spoken.
Won't ever matter if the few were once oppressed
Just listen to the Lord.

Moonlight will shine, take its place, as the beating sun
goes down.
Workers will travel to homes hoping there's some life around.
So let me listen…Just really Listen.
The Lord will guide me…bring forth His word.

So let's rejoice that the day brought
Another filling moment.
To thank Him for His blessings on the land
And we, as a people,
Should never disregard Him
The maker of it all, our lives so grand
Just listen to the Lord.

For He is there in the spotlight,
And my feet will travel His light…
to the kingdom of the chosen.
The ones He's blessed
But there are few who will listen
To the golden words well spoken.
Won't ever matter if the few were once oppressed
Just listen to the Lord.

The Light of
the Lord**

Come to the entrance the door will open
For those who seek…
Magic aside the miracle happens
For those who keep
Wanting some help with the fruits of a wonderful life
He'll give you strength as you cast aside all your strife.

Take of the hand to awaken your soul
For the wonders above let it take full control of you…
Come be a part and you'll forever live in the…
Light of the Lord

Live with His words for the beauty surrounds you
Throughout the day
Mindful of people , respect for your neighbor,
Bring kindness His way
Seek of the fortunes the Lord will bring as you live your life
Take the hand of your brothers and join in the gift of His
light

Take of the hand to awaken your soul
For the wonders above let it take full control of you…
Come be a part and you'll forever live in the…
Light of the Lord

For Him I Sing**

As I walk alone down the streets in the daylight
I hear of a lone voice
Who tells me to stay right
The calling to me just to follow the words of the Lord

My soul it is bursting with sounds of His laughter
The joy of the gift
The hope I was after
His teaching to me, He tells me to bring forth His word

Be patient boy
He tells me so
His righteousness
Of this I know
To walk with Him
His gift to bring
Resounding joy
For Him I sing

Let's bring forth the others, we'll all walk together
The work He has given
We're saying forever
His patience is full and His hope it is truly fulfilled

The masses are hearing. Messiah is calling
Let's turn from the evil
A brotherhood molding
We'll sing for the Lord the sounds of the music instilled

Be patient boy
He tells me so
His righteousness
Of this I know
To walk with Him
His gift to bring
Resounding joy
For Him I sing

(A Season)
Rejoicing my Life

Morning, I will try to remember
What I dreamed in my slumber
Were the gifts all from you?

Daylight, as I follow my footsteps
To the paths full of glory
There's a story of truth, I'll pursue

All the reasons for being
I know I'll be seeing
The realms of my passion in full colored fashion
The ones who will guide me
I feel right beside me
I've given my statement of life.

'Though dark was my vision,
A backwards decision
I'm told to awaken the inner sensation
Give up all my swerving
And know I'm deserving my right
A season rejoicing my life.

Evening, 'been a day fresh with changes
Attitude rearranges
And my outlook is bright.

Nighttime, I look forward to dreaming
My desires and scenery
All the colors and hues, the true sights

All the reasons for being
I know I'll be seeing
The realms of my passion in full colored fashion
The ones who will guide me
I feel right beside me
I've given my statement of life.

'Though dark was my vision,
A backwards decision
I'm told to awaken the inner sensation
Give up all my swerving
And know I'm deserving my right
A season rejoicing my life.

Be Patient

I was sitting, meditating,
Just relaxing heart and mind.
I was walking along the edge of the Universal line.
'Til I heard a voice just telling me
Discern from right and wrong
There are laws of understanding, this is where you belong.

Somebody hold me and teach me what I need
Somebody guide me, detach me from the greed
Emanate feelings that open up my mind
Somebody tell me Be Patient and be kind.

So the voice explained the rules to me
As it was since we've been born
Open up your heart, forgive, let go of hate and be strong
Send a message to the masses
That the peace can and will prevail
If we all respect each other, the Devil's hate is not for sale

Somebody hold me and teach me what I need
Somebody guide me, detach me from the greed
Emanate feelings that open up my mind
Somebody tell me Be Patient and be kind.
I can see my body down below as relaxed as it could be
And it drank in all the teachings that the Lord had told to me

So you can love and you can hate,
But the hate can cost too much
And destruction can follow you way beyond your mortal
touch
It's better to live a Godly life
The reward's are in your hand
And it's not just now, your future's bright, if you will just
comprehend

Somebody hold me and teach me what I need
Somebody guide me, detach me from the greed
Emanate feelings that open up my mind
Somebody tell me Be Patient and be kind.

Come into
my House

Come into my house
Hear the words of the Lord
Come into my house
Let us put down the sword
For there our eyes
Will be able to tear
Come into my house
The word of God we'll hear

Come into my house
For shelter we'll give
The cold outside
Is not for children to live
A good hot meal
Will soothe the craving inside
We all belong to the Lord
Let's drop our walls of pride

Come into my house
Let's rejoice in His name
Come into my house
He can hear all our shame
We'll build a new world
One of peace and of love
Come into my house
We'll bless the Lord above

Destiny's Soul

Sound of the trumpets that blew in the night
Yes there were beatings of drums before light
Violins playing to echo the tune
My voice was singing its richness in bloom

Thank all the angels that watch over me
Once there was darkness but now I can see
I understand all the crooked roads walked
Knowing the highways I'll talk…

Only 'bout love in my heart and that I want to know
How a little more patience can make my soul grow
Into finally reaching my ultimate goal
And completing my Destiny's Soul

So the orchestra played 'til the sun showed its rays
And the angels applauded what seemed to be days
And the lessons I've learned let my heart burst with joy
For I knew that my next step, a much harder ploy

Soon the music was back and the crowd stood to cheer
They were waiting for music and knew what they'd hear
That the tests were all passed and the grades were all in
And a concert was soon to begin

Only 'bout love in my heart and that I want to know
How a little more patience can make my soul grow
Into finally reaching my ultimate goal
And completing my Destiny's Soul

Forever Again

Listening and then talkin', while I'm standing then walkin'
On a Sunday afternoon
Getting ready for an evening, a new sermon and believing
Humming new or old tunes

Taking in some scenery, while the meditation seems to be
Calming my day's frustration
Opening all of my desires, feeling I am rewired
For a new week's presentation

Oh this is what I'm feeling. It's not magic when you're reeling
Inspired by the warmth of His touch
And the message that's delivered, and the skin when it shivers
Shivers when you know you're in His clutch
This is all around me, and my aura is astounding me
This is forever, Forever Again

While I was discerning, what I truly was learning
Would I succeed or would I fail
Did I want to change directions? Erase my negative conceptions
Lead my goodness to prevail

Oh this is what I'm feeling. It's not magic when you're reeling
Inspired by the warmth of His touch
And the message that's delivered, and the skin when it shivers
Shivers when you know you're in His clutch
This is all around me, and my aura is astounding me
This is forever, Forever Again

For the lessons are repeating to make sure we're not retreating
To a place we've already seen
We keep following emotions instead of breathing in the
notions
That the future is pristine

Oh this is what I'm feeling. It's not magic when you're reeling
Inspired by the warmth of His touch
And the message that's delivered, and the skin when it shivers
Shivers when you know you're in His clutch
This is all around me, and my aura is astounding me
This is forever, Forever Again

Friend of the Family

You feel you're alone again
There's no one in sight
Just look deep inside yourself
You'll soon see the light
Like raising your head up high
And into the night
A friend of the family
A good friend for life

You won't walk the streets again
Feel you're dragging your feet
Your energy level raised
You overcome your defeat
Just stretch to the highest star
You'll glow 'cause it's right
Your friend of the family
Your good friend for life

Just call on Him always
Whenever you feel you need a hand
And trust Him, believe in Him
Know that it's good to feel this grand

You're here with that special one
You know there is strength
The force that is guiding you
Will go to great lengths
You marvel the harmony
It's destiny's sight
The friend of the family
A good friend for life.

So know that He's there for all
No matter how, why or when
The friend of the family
The greatest of men

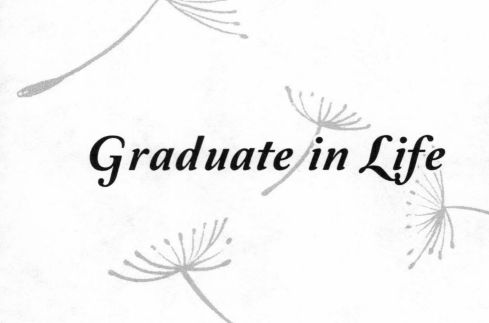

Graduate in Life

For all the times I heard the music in my mind
For all the hours that I've spent
With words to rhyme
For all the days I seem to care
And wonder where I'll be this time
I know that You are guiding me in life

For every minute that I need to understand
For every chapter, book and verse
That passed through my hand
For each new moment that will be,
I know that eventually
I'll see the reason, the cause for me in life

I wonder what the future has in store
For all who seek the truth
The real folklore
And yet to know that God within will bring forth only love
Let's search to seek the knowledge on this day
His rise above

Let's all embrace and pray to Him within our soul
In every lesson that we learn,
We strive to hold
And in the end we know it's time
And there is nothing to dislike
I know I'll pass and Graduate In Life

He'll Be There

He'll be there to comfort you throughout the day
He'll be there to aide your needs in any way
Understand that when you call
His ears will listen to it all
And all you have to do is sit and pray

Call to Him and He'll be there when you are down
Call to Him, He'll tell you how to turn it around
If you listen to your inner voice
And give yourself the choices
You will realize the hope that you have found

See the chances that you get throughout your life
Hear the calling in your inner ears delight
Smell the wonder of the world
As its beauty does unfurl
Touch the graces of His will the strength of His might

Be an active part the miracles we'll see
Be an active part our goals are harmony
Spread His consciousness to all
People calling want to share
Feel the glow that's in your heart.
He'll Be There!

The Higher Road

There are no roads I'll never travel on
My journey's taken an easy stride
But be aware of those whose strengths are gone
Just listen to your inner guides
I'm working for a purpose, my final goal
Erasing former faults within my soul

With every passing season
And every heartened reason
I'm destined to complete my tasks
And walk towards blessed passage
Secure that single message
Your good will conquer and be strong
There is no reason for being
Unless you are believing
The Higher Road to travel on

I'll stand up to all evils confronting me
I know the difference from right and wrong
The fire's burning for the world to see
Let's flush the embers and move on
A better path would be to love mankind
To walk with kindred eyes and not be blind

With every passing season
And every heartened reason
I'm destined to complete my tasks
And walk towards blessed passage
Secure that single message
Your good will conquer and be strong
There is no reason for being
Unless you are believing
The Higher Road to travel on

The House of God

It is a hope
It is a dream I've always wished for
It is a place that I've always yearned to be
It is a time
A certain era that I've longed for
And yet my heart knows for sure I'll never see

It is a wonder for the mind
To think and crave those brilliant times
When we're all together
In the House of God
For this is how the world should be
In peaceful joy, serenity
And we're loving all
And in the House of God

I've always felt that empty loneliness
Inside of me
I've always looked and have searched for answers sure
And for a time
I really thought I'd never find it
Until the light beamed a beacon bright and pure

It is a wonder for the mind
To think and crave those brilliant times
When we're all together
In the House of God
For this is how the world should be
In peaceful joy, serenity
And we're loving all
And in the House of God

I Go Out of
my Mind

You are a blessing for me
Sent from the one I consider the source
And now that our paths are together
We know there could never be
Nothing, but harmony

So let us now work two as one
Showing our spirits have joined as a team
Let's embrace all our fears
And to shed all our tears
Knowing clouds have dispersed with the sun

For I go out of my mind with your laughter
And I go out of my mind when you smile
A feeling that touches the soul
I am out of control
I was longing for you for awhile

And I wish all of our dreams and passions
Will melt the stress and the troubles away
I hope that there would never be
Any mountain or sea
To divide any reason to say…
I go out of my mind for you
I go out of my mind

'Though there's the chance for discourse
Let us consider this only a test
For we know the triumph ahead
As we peel back the dread
Will enlighten our soul's inner source

There's strength in the number we share
To double can only enhance what we have
For all of the care and concern
Is His will as we learn
Brings us truth as we unfold and bear

For I go out of my mind with your laughter
And I go out of my mind when you smile
A feeling that touches the soul
I am out of control
I was longing for you for awhile

And I wish all of our dreams and passions
Will melt the stress and the troubles away
I hope that there would never be
Any mountain or sea
To divide any reason to say...
I go out of my mind for you
I go out of my mind

Just Understand

I want. I need.
I crave. I'll heed.
The words.
The message of the Lord.
I'll search. I'll find.
I'll learn. I'll mind.
The laws and the written word of God.

For there's a rich old history
And knowledge we should know,
Let's learn from past mistakes
And let us grow.

Let's stop. Let it sink in.
In terms of what the cause will have…
And if we harm our fellow man.
Just know that what we give
Will return the gift from Him
And know the law is just.
Just Understand

Lately

Lately, I am believing
That the gifts I've been receiving
Are the blessings and good tidings
From above.
Lately, 'cause you are with me
I'm no longer lonely
And there's peace within me
I see all directions and strive for perfections
And bring forth more love

And oh walk with me
Be part of the school of life that I long and seek
That will credit rewards in my time
And oh the evils will fade
If we seek for the best
All the faults and the tests of mankind.

Lately, the chores I've been given
I try to do without misgivings
I am grateful
And cast away hateful thoughts I might bare
Lately, 'though I walk stately
I am only modest
But know I am honest
To do what's asked of me without begrudging
Be kind and to care

And oh walk with me
Let me be part of the school of life
That I need to learn and be free
And oh bring me relief
'Cause the tests are amassing, I know I am passing
With grades to bring me degrees.

Lately, I am believing
That the gifts I've been receiving
Are the blessings and good tidings
From above.
Lately, 'cause you are with me
I'm no longer lonely
And if there's peace within me
I see all directions and strive for perfections
And bring forth more love

Love, Hope
and Prayer

Love shouldn't be a heart wrenching hurt
Love shouldn't walk out
Should never desert
It should only build throughout the years
Love is a goal
With laughter and tears

Hope is a dream of all ages of life
Hope gives you wings
To guide you through flight
It lets you become the things that you dream
With love by its side,
It flows like a stream

For whatever rhymes or reasons there may be
We can't change the past, but only see
And the future can reflect serenity
If we live with love, hope and harmony

Prayer is the source for one and all
Prayer is the strength
Won't ever let you fall
Believe in your hopes and love with raise the tide
For prayer is the code
Your road map and guide.

Oh, this is Love

I can hardly explain the miracles that I've pictured in my
mind
But I know these treasured imagined things
Will never waste my time
I can only thank the Lord above for the images I've seen
It's a blessing for the world to know
the places that I've been
Don't you ever tell me I am wrong
That I waste the entire day
You don't know the things inside of me
Or the words I need to say

And it used to be
Kind of like a symphony
Playing all the music
From the heavens up above
I only want to see the light
A kind of philharmonic sight
Oh, This is Love.

As each morning comes I am inspired to open up my mind
And to listen to my inner voice
The gifts that I shall find
I can always count on Him for life, my partnership with Thee
And the teachers that have been assigned
To guide a better me
Don't you understand the words I sing?
Just listen with your heart.
And feel the warmth inside yourself.
Today is life's new start

And it used to be
Kind of like a symphony
Playing all the music
From the heavens up above
I only want to see the light
A kind of philharmonic sight
Oh, This is Love.

Bring forth a brand new day
Believe in the things I have to say

And it used to be
Kind of like a symphony
Playing all the music
From the heavens up above
I only want to see the light
A kind of philharmonic sight
Oh, This is Love.

The Odyssey

It had started with the dawn of time
On a hot and humid day
There was nothing left for us to climb
There was nothing in our way
Then He ushered in the mountains high
Soon a river there would flow
And a story would begin to rhyme
Was so very long ago.
And the paths we took we knew were great.
Was the first of many tests.
Didn't know if we were right or wrong
Didn't know when we should rest

We believed it was the Odyssey
There were many twists and turns
And the population grew so fast
Only few would care to yearn
For the knowledge and the gifts of One
For the longing to go home
There were more who simply didn't care
Selfish attitudes were shown
So they needed to begin anew
Now knowing there's another chance
And to follow forth just like those few
Who didn't need another glance

So begins another Odyssey
Another life the same old tests.
Maybe this time we would pass them all
Show Him we're the very best
All the rules and regulated laws
All the footnotes from the past
Let us hope to build a "Heavened" world
One where God will surely last.
And when it's time to leave our present plane
Rise above the soul complete
We will know that we have grown with time
Begin the next phase of our feat.

We are on another Odyssey
Another destined Oyssey.

On a Permanent Basis

We are here you see, as it's meant to be
There are reasons for our life
For the record shows, as our story goes
When we learn it no longer cuts like a knife

Though the path's not straight, it won't have to wait
For the goal is to be a righteous one
In the end we'll know if we have to sow
Or to reap rewards and not live another life as we had just
done

Let me fly to You
On a permanent basis
Let me sing for You
Give of myself
Let me run to You
To the beauty of your arms
So the world can see that eternity's really true
On a permanent basis with You

The regrets we've made, mend what's been so frayed
'Takes a long time to heal
Let our thoughts be good, teach of brotherhood
Bring the flock in for one meal

In the end we'll see God's security
And a light that brightens as it grows
Let the truth be known, we're never on our own
For the soul knows the steps to take, its guidance tells us so

Let me fly to You
On a permanent basis
Let me sing for You
Give of myself
Let me run to You
To the beauty of your arms
So the world can see that eternity's really true
On a permanent basis with You

I Won't Have
to Choose

Whether I'm happy
Sad or just feeling blue
I know that there's a place I can go
Be with you
Pick up my spirits
Go on and continue on to follow not lose
There's no doubt about it
With You I won't have to choose

Follow directions
Day in and day out I'm torn
Whether I go or stay in the places
That make me feel worn
Daydreaming fever
Wonder if I've really blown a fuse
But I know my place
I'm with You and I won't have to choose

I won't have to think about the love in my heart for you
Or the goals that I've set
And the promises made in my mind
And the classes that I take to learn the lessons and expand
Will I pass the tests that I take
A better mankind

Back to the present
Ready to take on my blues
'Though work is a hassle
I'd rather spend my time with You
Get through the day
So I can be closer never to misconstrue
You're all that I need
I know that I won't have to choose

There's no doubt about it
With You, I won't have to choose

Our Message
from Above

Everybody's talking through me
Telling me I should be happy
All the time
I want to understand the feelings
Listen to my rhymes and reasons
Won't be blind

Simple laws and such devotions
Thinking of the mixed emotions
Standing there
Isn't life a misconception?
Deep in thought of all direction
Feeling bare

But everybody wants a piece of time
Thinking that I'm full of plenty
Being kind
But missing You is always on my mind
I am searching and wanting You

And don't you feel the wishes of your family
Can't you see we just want to be so free
Let us learn what we need to be
It's our Message from Above

Peace to be His goal with loving
Call out to the mass
Send thoughts of all His deeds
Read to them the thoughts of wisdom
Vision life amongst His Kingdom
If you heed

But everybody wants a piece of time
Thinking that I'm full of plenty
Being kind
But missing You is always on my mind
I am searching and wanting You

And don't you feel the wishes of your family
Can't you see we just want to be so free
Let us learn what we need to be
It's our Message from Above

The Reasons
for His Life

Open your eyes to your dreams and seek the wonder
And the power of the mind
Open your ears to world of sounds so clear
And soon you will find
Open your heart give this world a chance
For peace to grow
And let us dance
In the knowledge
And the Reasons for His Life

Open your mind to all challenges and be
The best that you can
Open your hand and shake up the world
Let's rejoice with your fellow man
Open your heart to the ones who are
Less able than you
Who stand from afar
And show them
The Reasons for His Life

For He wanted to show
That kindness bring kindness
That love can grow
And He wanted to bring
The messages
That we should all sing

Open the door to the ones in need
And offer whatever you can
Open the gate and give of yourself
For peace and love is at hand
Open a world full of doubts and regrets
Let's turn it around
And let us beget
The knowledge
And the Reasons for His life

Real Truth

We exist for one goal
To have and to hold
There's more to life than we see
Record all our faults
Successes and jolts
The reason to grow and be free
For life travels fast
And we need to grasp
The causes for being this way
We hope to succeed
We strive to pass
While we play

There's a fire down deep in my soul
And it's burning throughout
My desire to let you know
That our paths have crossed
There's no doubt
So we look at the skies
Search for stars in our eyes
But only see the proof
With Him at our side
We know that we'll have Real Truth

Won't overstep bounds
While searching the grounds
It's good to go by the rules
The traps there have been
Avoiding the sin
Effects would enhance being cruel
By learning to love
Hold tight with our glove
The fruits will be our rewards
Won't ever regret
The goals we have met
Thank the Lord

There's a fire down deep in my soul
And it's burning throughout
My desire to let you know
That our paths have crossed
There's no doubt
So we look at the skies
Search for stars in our eyes
But only see the proof
With Him at our side
We know that we'll have Real Truth

The Rest of my Life with You

We are standing here today
We are ready to start our brand new lives
As we speak our vows and say
Make the promises to become husband and wife
This is moment that we've been waiting for
This is God's gift
Our paths have crossed before

Let us take the steps we need to walk
Fulfill our destined road
To become the best we strive to be
And meet what's been foretold
I want to lift my glass
Give thanks for the prayers so true
I want to spend my time
The Rest of My Life with You

We've begun to see the light
We've been blessed for all the good that we stand for
With our hearts forever bright
We will gleen the truth, stand steadfast evermore
This is the moment to look into our souls
Live in God's righteousness
The truths are what we hold

Let us take the steps we need to walk
Fulfill our destined road
To become the best we strive to be
And meet what's been foretold
I want to lift my glass
Give thanks for the prayers so true
I want to spend my time
The Rest of My Life with You

For the miracles He gives us
His love's and endless land
And we will never forsaken
The ring upon our hands

Let us take the steps we need to walk
Fulfill our destined road
To become the best we strive to be
And meet what's been foretold
I want to lift my glass
Give thanks for the prayers so true
I want to spend my time
The Rest of My Life with You

Singing Praise Hallelujah

There are bells ringing loud
To the joy of the crowd
Singing praise hallelujah to Thee
And the people they dance
To the tune of romance
Singing praise hallelujah to Thee

Sing of good. Sing of right
Hear the music's delight
It' a calling for all to be near
For together we're strong
We know where we belong
And His message comes through crystal clear.

Close our eyes let us see
What the soul's meant to be
There's the path we should for all time
If we follow the steps
We will cancel our debts
And be closer to being divine

Let's erase all our hate
Learn to love, not berate
Singing praise hallelujah to Thee
We will grow and we'll bless
All the negative stress
Singing praise hallelujah to Thee

Close our eyes let us see
What the soul's meant to be
There's the path we should for all time
If we follow the steps
We will cancel our debts
And be closer to being divine

There are bells ringing loud
To the joy of the crowd
Singing praise hallelujah to Thee
And the people they dance
To the tune of romance
Singing praise hallelujah to Thee

We will grow and we'll bless
All the negative stress
Singing praise hallelujah to Thee

We're here at last
We begin to see the morning light
Our eyes are opened
Sun feels right
It's distinct and so exact
And what we hear
Are the sounds the gifts from only One
To behold the noises
Life's begun
Will enhance they don't distract

So hold on tight
This ride's too short
The life we lead
To bring us forth
Our vision's clear
We can see the picture full of colored hues
We won't deny
Our trouble past
We're here right now
To break the grasp
Let's live as one
For there is one thing on this earth I'd rather do
Is Spend My Life for You

We mustn't fall
There's a price to pay for lessons failed
Like a debt for others to assail
Take a different point of view
With a kind and gentle word
We can turn around an angry crowd
And to let them know we cry out loud
For it's love we will pursue

So hold on tight
This ride's too short
The life we lead
To bring us forth
Our vision's clear
We can see the picture full of colored hues
We won't deny
Our trouble past
We're here right now
To break the grasp
Let's live as one
For there is one thing on this earth I'd rather do
Is Spend My Life for You

This is Heaven Here on Earth

So I close my eyes and meditate
Wishing for the joy of Heaven's gate to see
To be one with You forevermore
Knowing You would never close the door to me
This is glory, the love of my life
Like a ship that is sailing to the stars in the night
Picture a moment without start or an end
To be hopelessly in Love

The wheels are set in motion
Moving dutifully around
Never thinking that the circle
Has to finish with a sound
There is nothing here to stop
Just continue never drop
Like an atom at its birth

We're His glory and His passion
Bring us back into the fold
We were perfect from beginning
Like the source, we're the mold
Let the mountains and trees
Meld with powers from the seas
Let the beauty show its worth
This is Heaven Here on Earth

To eclipse the sun is just a test
With our patience we can see His best. Let's shout!
Whether small or large it does not need
To be vilified with little seeds of doubt
We're in the closing last chapter of the book
Let us remember if the story had the hook
Open our mind to the vastness of the time
We are hopelessly in love

The wheels are set in motion
Moving dutifully around
Never thinking that the circle
Has to finish with a sound
There is nothing here to stop
Just continue never drop
Like an atom at its birth
We're His glory and His passion
Bring us back into the fold

We were perfect from beginning
Like the source, we're the mold
Let the mountains and trees
Meld with powers from the seas
Let the beauty show its worth
This is Heaven Here on Earth

Tomorrow's Joy

This whole world seems big and bright
Hoping all will soon see the light
I've been waiting around too long
Looking for that someone to take me on board and sing the
song
of God's reward
I should discover what He gave
Why we should cover all the past and its mistakes
To learn from them it's what will make
Tomorrow's joy

Listen to the sounds of your heart
Telling you to be a part
Give to one who needs a hand
Help a child that wants and seeks to strive and understand
It's God's reward
He will discover what He gave
Why we should cover life and limb the start of all
His message clear we're one for all
Tomorrow's Joy

Hope and harmony
We all need
Plant that seed to mend
And let us build to learn and bend

125

This big world is getting small
Let's forgive stand straight and tall
Reason out forsaken ills
Enlighten all to shine, let's walk the path and bring good will
for God's reward
We will discover what He gave
Why we should cover healing wounds and troubled souls
The glory of the one who holds
All the past and its mistakes
To learn from them it's what it takes
Life and limb the start of all
His message clear we're one for all of
Tomorrow's Joy

With you Back
in my Life

Didn't hardly understand
Want to run away and hide
Wasn't feeling so complete
Didn't feel that good inside
'Stead of running far away
I confronted all the strife
It was good to be back home
And with You back in my life

So we will talk and we'll listen
To the changing of the winds
And we'll harmonize just like we were one
Giving thanks for all the gifts
Just like the Son

Should I romp around your garden
Stop and smell the sweet perfume
It was part of the big picture
Ocean breezes and sand dunes
There are times of graduation
Rising to the next plateau
Taking each step as it's given
Part of being in the know

So we'll talk and we'll listen
To the words we need to hear
And a union only builds stronger bonds
For the lessons we hold dear

Didn't hardly understand
Didn't want to compromise
Couldn't comprehend emotions
Running 'fore my very eyes
I felt humbled conversation
No one throwing any knives
It was good to be back home
And with You back in my life

Bring Forth

Bring forth the name of the Lord
To the house of the sinner
Bring forth his Godly ways
And let him repent
Give him the Lords commandments
And tell him he's not a winner
Until he turns from his evil ways
And is Heaven's sent

Let's turn off the music
That only speaks of destruction
Let's set aside the words that hurt our fellow man
Create a world for all
To live with positive construction
And build a place for all to join our hands

Bring forth the name of the Lord
To the house of the sinner
Bring forth his Godly ways
And let him repent
Give him the Lords commandments
And tell him he's not a winner
Until he turns from his evil ways
And is Heaven's sent

I'm tired of reading
About the crimes near our homes
It makes me feel and wonder where's the good in us all
Let's fill the world
With only positive words not stones
Be humble and help the tired and meek who would fall

Bring forth the name of the Lord
To the house of the sinner
Bring forth his Godly ways
And let him repent
Give him the Lords commandments
And tell him he's not a winner
Until he turns from his evil ways
And is Heaven's sent

I'm Getting Stronger

I never thought I had meaning in my life
I never thought that anyone cared
I'd go through each day wondering how I'd see it end
And if there were others who just stared.

But you came along and showed me the way
You taught me how to be a friend
We read through the book of holiness
We tell the Lord we comprehend

I've been afraid for so long
For being in darkness not knowing wrong
Yet asking for time
No forgiveness in my life
And still I can pray
And ask of the Lord
To show me what's right
Fulfilling His word
'Cause I'm Getting Stronger
And loving the Lord again

Now you and I are believers
We stand for the truth the ultimate way
There's no wrong in denying our past
We've learned how to hope, forgive and to pray

There's more who need to hear the word
There's more who want to know His way
So let's stand together as one family
Let's reach for the Lord as we say

I've been afraid for so long
For being in darkness not knowing wrong
Yet asking for time
No forgiveness in my life
And still I can pray
And ask of the Lord
To show me what's right
Fulfilling His word
'Cause I'm Getting Stronger
And loving the Lord again

For His Love

Rest ye good ones
All ye servants
Of His word
All the children and the hungry
Shall be heard
For tomorrow there's rejoicing
In the kingdom of the Lord
Rest ye good ones
All ye servants
Of His word

For the servants
Who comfort
Those in pain
All the martyrs who hath given
In His name
For tomorrow hear the calling
To His Heaven up above
Take the sunlight
Touch the bright light
Of His love

He will rule forever
Your soul belong to Him
Give Him praise
Confess your sins
His light will never dim

Rest ye good ones
All ye who speak
His word
In your hardships overcome
Through the Lord
For tomorrow our future
Lies in Heaven
Up above
Rest ye good ones
All ye servants
All ye children
And the hungry
All ye servants
Who cry out
For His Love

To Live with Thee

My hands are weak
My knees they shake
I'm trembling from the thrill
My chattering teeth
My sweaty palms
I get excited, I chill
I'm all aglow
And now I know
That life won't pass me by
'Cause every time
I pray to the Lord
I know He's there beside

He's there beside me
He's all around
I live for Him
My prayers abound
Forgive my sins
I ask of Thee
My eternal soul
To Live With Thee

Jesus died
So we could live
We'd never forget His deed
We owe it to
The Holy Father
To ask we shall receive
And in return
Our lives for Him
We'll live by His commands
Our neighbors we'll love
We'll bless the day
In unity we'll stand

He's there beside me
He's all around
I live for Him
My prayers abound
Forgive my sins
I ask of Thee
My eternal soul
To Live With Thee

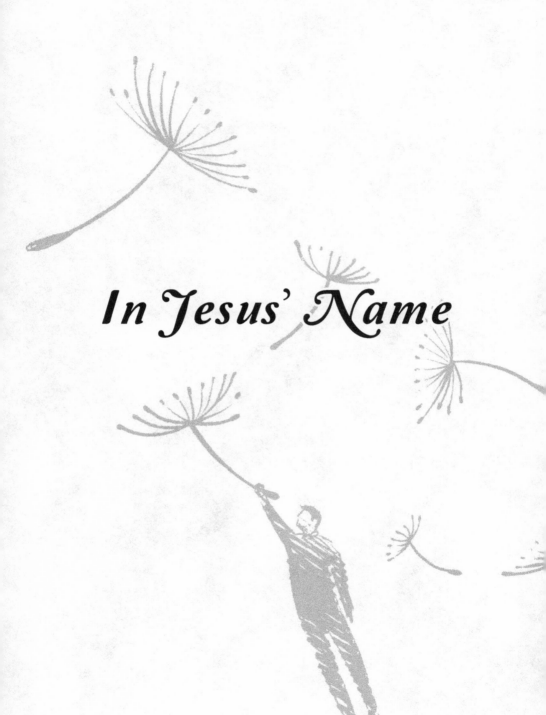

In Jesus' Name

I will worship in Jesus' name
I will take in the words like falling rain
I will drink in the rain like it's sweet wine
I will worship until the end of time

Yes Jesus is the one
He's the Lord
My shining sun
There's no other in my life
And I am free from all the strife
With Jesus I am blessed
When He calls
I'll face the test
For I'll only worship
In Jesus' name

I will tell those who've yet to find the Lord
They will search and examine His word
Those who seek will have questions answered all
With Jesus they will stand straight and tall

Yes Jesus is the one
He's the Lord
My shining sun
There's no other in my life
And I am free from all the strife
With Jesus I am blessed
When He calls
I'll face the test
For I'll only worship
In Jesus' name

And the Witness is This

And the witness is this
That God has given us eternal life
And the life's in His son
And the witness is this
If we have the Son
We have the life
If we do not have the Son of the Lord
We won't have the life
And the witness is this

We should all give thanks
For His glorious deeds
And the world He gave
We should all meet His needs
For His only Son
Who chose to pursue
A life full of prayer for me and for you
We should all give thanks
For His glorious deeds

Time is on His side
He will live forever
Love should be our guide
A promise for better
So to call on the Lord
We'll do this each and every day
Give prayer to Him
Have fear in Him
Believe in Him
Revere in Him

And the witness is this
That God has given us eternal life
And the life's in His son
And the witness is this
If we have the Son
We have the life
If we do not have the Son of the Lord
We won't have the life
And the witness is this

You are the One

I sing for you every night I know you're here
I read your words from your book I hold so dear
I worship you every night and every day
I know that you will never walk away

'Cause You are the One who takes my hurt
Turns it around and makes it good
And You are the One who knows
That I am not misunderstood
And You are the One who keeps me warm
With your shining sun
There won't be another
"Cause You are the One

A simple tune and the words you give to me
A precious love that no one would ever see
A silent thought that I give to only you
A peaceful moment just between we two

'Cause You are the One who takes my hurt
Turns it around and makes it good
And You are the One who knows
That I am not misunderstood
And You are the One who keeps me warm
With your shining sun
There won't be another
"Cause You are the One

A prayer I say just before I go to sleep
That quiet time is the moment that I keep
The day was full with the work you gave to me
My life for You for this is how it must be

'Cause You are the One who takes my hurt
Turns it around and makes it good
And You are the One who knows
That I am not misunderstood
And You are the One who keeps me warm
With your shining sun
There won't be another
"Cause You are the One

The Wind and His Grace

Shadows from the wind
It's your destiny that calls
Can you answer from your past?
Do you know your troubled alls?

Is your story fully told?
Is it rich with buried oil?
Are the ghosts that bear your sins
Repaid with karmic soil?

Do you question why the goodness of God
Or take for granted all His love?
We should give back what we feel from the heart
Our rewards we'll reap from whence we first start

Alone we'll figure out
What our story really is
We will meditate for truth
Pure light is gentle bliss

When it's time we'll know it all
All the answers to the wind
We can then ask for His grace
All our harmony will blend

Do you question why the goodness of God
Or take for granted all His love?
We should give back what we feel from the heart
Our rewards we'll reap from whence we first start

In my daily readings of scripture, the following presented a perfect end to this book of poetry or prose, however the reader decides to interpret.

3 Corinthians 5:6-10
We are always courageous, although we know that while we are at home in the body we are away from the Lord,
For we walk by faith, not by sight. Yet we are courageous, and would rather leave the body and go home to the Lord.
Therefore, we aspire to please him, whether we are at home or away. For we must appear before the judgment
seat of Christ, so that each one may receive recompense, according to what he did in the body, whether good or evil.

I actually find this passage in 3 Corinthians terrifying. How many truly look to the past for the deeds they did or did not do. And if they realize, if they are believers, their perspectives on their daily actions should be altered in the course of doing what is just and right.

Today's times are challenging. Most of it is reactionary and completed without true thought of learning from the past. Unfortunately, mankind, and womankind, are destined to repeat the same mistakes.

I just pray and hope that our choices can be made for a better world. God gave us so much. How horrible it would be to destroy it all for vanity and riches.